A Furry-Tale Life

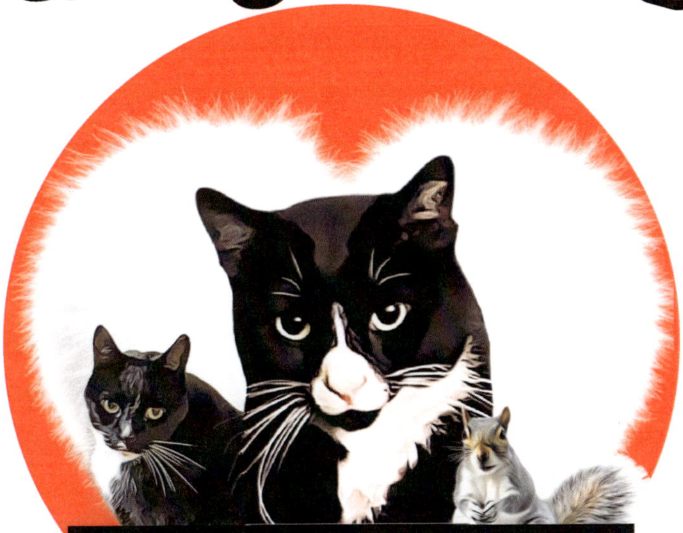

Baby, The Rescue Kitty's Journey to His Forever Family

Hi there, animal lovers! My name is Baby, The Rescue Kitty. Ten years ago, someone moved out of their house and left me behind in the mountains of California. My story had a happy conclusion but sadly, many companion animals face abandonment every year. I hope this book shines a light on kindness towards our furry friends and the importance of humane education for kids.

Warm purrs and lots of love,
Baby, The Rescue Kitty.

First Edition 2024
Published by Kelly Fallucca, Sugar Please Productions
Edited by Hallie Lagestee and Bryony van der Merwe

Sugar Please Productions, LLC

Copyright © 2024 by Kelly Fallucca, founder of Sugar Please Productions, LLC

All rights reserved.

Printed in the United States of America. Without the written permission of the publisher, one may not reproduce, store, or transmit any part of this publication in any form or by any means.

The images in this book are real-life photos that the author has cartooned and digitally composited. Kelly Fallucca produced the entire production, including the cover art, script, and imagery.

Final Edit by Hallie Lagestee
First Edit by Bryony van der Merwe

Sugar Please Productions - www.SugarPleaseProductions.com

Contact at: k@sugarpleaseproductions.com

First Edition 2024
ISBN: 979-8-9866407-2-3
Library of Congress Control Number: 2024904648

Dedication

I dedicate this book to all the animal lovers around the world who support and care for our furry friends. Baby is one of the great loves of my life and I am privileged to share his story.

To our dear friends and family who cheered us on throughout this long journey, your contributions have been invaluable.

A special thank you to Jane Gissi, Mike Madden, Hallie Lagestee, Lilly Rose, Connie Pedenko, Mara Williams, Lynne Dauenhauer, and Jean Tracy for their significant impact on my life and this project.

And finally, to my parents, who always believed in my creativity even when I doubted it. Thank you!

On behalf of Baby and myself, we love you all!
– XOXO, Kelly & Baby –

One day, someone abandoned a little kitty in the mountains of California. The kitty meowed and meowed, but no one came. As it grew dark and cold, tears started flowing from his eyes. "Why did they leave me?" the kitty wondered sadly.

He heard a scratching in the tree above him.

"Hello, my name is Chunky," said the squirrel.

The kitten softly replied, "I don't have a name."

Chunky expressed sympathy for the kitty. "Don't worry, there are lots of houses near here. I'll bet one of them will be your forever family."

"What's a forever family?" asked the curious kitty.

"I'll explain in the morning," said Chunky. "Let's get some sleep. Tomorrow, we will look for your new family."

"Okay," said the kitten, falling asleep in a bed of leaves.

"Good morning, kitty!" Chunky exclaimed.

"What!?" the startled kitty yelped, as he had fallen asleep so deeply that he had forgotten where he was when he awoke.

"It's time to find you a family," Chunky reminded him.

"Look, over there, those people look nice, and they have a kitty in the window that looks just like you!" exclaimed Chunky.

The hopeful kitty looked over and saw three nice looking people standing in front of the house: Jane, Mikey, and Kelly.

Jane, the woman with the dark hair, said, "Is that the kitty we saw as we passed the abandoned house last week?"

"He is the one," said the man named Mikey.

The blonde woman named Kelly said, "He must be hungry."

Kelly went into the house and came back with a snack for the kitty.

"It is okay. We will take care of you," she told him gently.

"Can we keep him, Mikey?" Kelly asked.

"We should ask the neighbors and contact the local shelter to check if anyone has lost a kitty first," suggested Mikey.

So that's what they did.

While Mikey and Jane spoke to the neighbors and hung posters, Kelly held the kitty tightly as he purred happily.

No one knew anything about the missing kitty, so the next day they took him to the local veterinarian.

"He's not micro-chipped," said the vet. "You can keep him if you want to."

Kelly hugged him tightly. "He's coming home with us."

The kitten purred happily! He couldn't wait to tell Chunky!

"What shall we name him?" asked Kelly.

Mikey said, "Let him settle in, and his name will reveal itself to us."

After they returned home, the kitty saw Chunky from the upstairs window.

"They want to keep me!" The kitty shouted.

Chunky smiled. "I knew they would."

"Thank you Chunky," said the kitty with a purr of gratitude.

Then Kelly came and picked him up from the window.
"It's bath time, kitty."

As she headed toward the sink, he realized
she wanted to put him in water.

"No, no, no, cats don't like water," said the kitty as he sat
quietly in the sink planning his escape.

Kelly eventually found them. As she knelt and looked under the table, she said, "It's okay, Fizz. I'm just going to bathe him, and then we can all cuddle up on the couch."

"I don't want a bath,"

said the kitty.

Fizz said, "I know, but you need to wash the dirt off from living outside. It will be okay. Trust me."

Fizz, wrapped in a fluffy towel, sat nervously by the kitty.
As Kelly made a bubble bath in the sink.

Kelly laughed, "Aww, Fizz, you're acting just like his mother.
Tell you what, we can share mama duties. He can be our baby."

Then she gasped, "That's it! We'll name him Baby."
Fizz asked the kitty. "What do you think? Do you like the name Baby?"

As they all snuggled on the couch, the kitten thought, "I have a name. Baby. I am Baby, The Rescue Kitty."
Then he fell asleep next to his new family, knowing he had found his forever family.

Thinking back on his journey, Baby realized, "Miracles really do happen."

Who would have thought a kitty left in the mountains would have a furry-tale life and a forever family?

Baby lived happily ever after.

The end.

Subscribe to My YouTube Channel For Educational Videos

www.ingramcontent.com/pod-product-compliance
Lightning Source LLC
LaVergne TN
LVRC090724070526
838199LV00019B/542